STORY OF AMERICA

Colonial America

Margaret Fisher
Mary Jane Fowler

Margaret Fisher is an author and editor of books for children. After graduating from Maryville College in Tennessee, she attended Mexico City College. As a public school teacher in Tennessee and in Michigan, Miss Fisher became keenly aware of the needs and interests of grade school children. Mary Jane Fowler is also an author and editor of children's textbooks. She attended Michigan State University and the University of Michigan. Mrs. Fowler made a special study of the colonial period in American history. These authors write about colonial life in a vivid, interesting style.

EDITORS AND ADVISORS

Curriculum Editor	Raymond E. Fideler
Associate Editor	David Proud
Manuscript Editors	Beverly Linsley
	Marion Smith
	Rene Schuyten
Index Editors	Hester Chase
	Lila Grace Beattie
Picture Editor	Beverly Linsley
Art Editor	Alan Adsmond
Map Editor	Ruth Wieda
Historical Editor	Dr. Alexander DeConde
	Associate Professor of History
	University of Michigan

STORY OF AMERICA

GREAT EXPLORERS   **PIONEER DAYS**

COLONIAL AMERICA   **TRANSPORTATION**

GREAT AMERICANS

COLONIAL AMERICA

Margaret Fisher
Mary Jane Fowler

THE FIDELER COMPANY - - GRAND RAPIDS, MICHIGAN

Grateful acknowledgement is made to the following for permission to use the illustrations found in this book:

Adrian Beerhorst: Paintings on pages 9, 11, 86, 92, 101, and 118.
Andrews: Page 24 (bottom).
Art Institute of Chicago: Page 26.
Bettmann Archive: Pages 64, 80, 87, and 106.
Boston Public Library: Pages 18 and 91.
Brown Brothers: Pages 70, 71, 83, 90, and 116.
Colonial Williamsburg: Pages 27, 37 (center), 41, 42, 43, 65, 66, 67, 107, 108, 109, 112, 113, 119, 120, and 123.
Compton's Pictured Encyclopedia: Page 63.
Cooper Union Museum: Pages 39 (top center) and 44 (left and center).
Cushing: Pages 47, 50, 53, and 105.
Devaney: Pages 25, 33, and 103.
Essex Institute: Page 39 (bottom).
First Baptist Church in America: Page 85.
Galloway: Page 97.
Gendreau: Page 55.
Harding: Page 17.
Harry Shaw Newman, Old Print Shop, Inc.: Page 45.
Historical Society of Pennsylvania: Page 29.
Illustrated London News: Page 14.
J. Horace McFarland Company: Page 40.
John Hancock Mutual Life Insurance Company: Page 74.
Library of Congress: Pages 20, 21, 23, 24 (top), 60, 69, 77, and 84.
McLaughlin: Page 61.
National Life Insurance Company: Pages 30, 31, 32, 48, 68, 75, 76, 82, 88, 94, 98, 99, and 110.
National Park Service, U. S. Department of the Interior: Pages 13, 102, and 111.
New England Mutual Life Insurance Company: Page 89.
New-York Historical Society: Page 124.
New York Public Library: Page 79.
Pilgrim Society: Page 16.
Plimoth Plantation Photo: Pages 3, 19, and 35.
Plymouth Antiquarian Society: Pages 49, 51, 52, 54, 56, 57, and 59.
Pocumtuck Valley Memorial Association: Pages 36 (all except center), 39 (left and right), and 44 (right).
Roberts: Page 28.
Smithsonian Institution: Pages 34, 36 (center), 37 (all except center), and 114.
Title Guarantee Company: Pages 15 from a painting by Edward L. Henry and 72 from a painting by John Ward Dunsmore.
United States Forest Service: Page 12.
Virginia State Chamber of Commerce: Pages 10 and 22.

TO THE TEACHER

A Better Way to Study Colonial America

Arouse Interest and Help Students Think.   Use five to ten copies of this *Colonial America* textbook and one copy of the portfolio of Classroom Pictures (loose-leaf edition of the book) to interest your students in learning more about the American colonists and how they lived.

Keep Children Thinking.   Divide the class into committees, each of which will seek answers to such questions as:

. . . For what reason did many of the first colonists come to North America?
. . . How did the colonists help each other?
. . . In what ways did people in Colonial America earn their living?

For its research work, let each committee use traditional textbooks and one or more copies of the *Colonial America* textbook, plus those chapters and pictures from the *Colonial America* portfolio that relate to the topic the committee is investigating. This easy-to-understand text, enriched with well-chosen pictures for each topic, makes learning much more effective. It speeds up the learning process and makes the students feel that they are being transplanted in imagination into the period of history they are studying.

Then let each committee present its most important findings to the whole class. The committee should be questioned by the rest of the class and the teacher. This procedure will provide an enriched learning experience.

Give Every Child a Chance to Think and Learn.   This *Colonial America* text-book is designed for use on three reading ability levels. (See next page.) When you use five to ten copies of this textbook and the matching port-folio of Classroom Pictures in the manner described above, you give every child a chance to think and learn. Slow learners, children with average abilities, and students with superior minds are able to find answers to their questions and form vivid mental images that are necessary for understand-ing this period of American history.

How to Meet the Learning Needs of Every Child

The editors of this book believe that the secret of successful learning lies in motivating the student to *think*. This fundamental principle has been effectively stated by John Dewey in his book *Democracy and Education:* "The sole path to enduring improvement in the methods of instruction and learning consists in centering upon the conditions which exact, promote, and test thinking. Thinking *is* the method of intelligent learning; of learning that employs and rewards the mind." Our great need is to lead students to think purposefully.

Purpose and Interest

Purpose and interest are the most important elements of thinking. To expect students to read and think about history without first helping them find a purpose, or an interest, is to invite their failure. The first step in teaching history should be to create a highly challenging environment that will arouse the natural curiosity of the students. The teacher may create this environment with the help of the proper learning aids. A good filmstrip or large pin-up-board pictures are powerful aids for creating interest and developing purpose on the part of the student. The clear, lighted pictures in a good filmstrip about Colonial America appeal to every student's natural curiosity. If a filmstrip or a collection of good pictures about life in Colonial America is not available, the teacher can group the students in such a way that the entire class may share more effectively all of the copies of this textbook that are in the classroom. If the attention of each member of the class is centered on the same picture at the same time, the students as a group can enjoy visual experiences that are almost as satisfactory as those made possible by a filmstrip or bulletin board display.

Successful motivation will bring forth a number of questions to which the class will want to find answers. These questions should be recorded, discussed, and revised by the group. Those that offer a true challenge to the students' efforts open the way for a profitable study of Colonial America.

[A portfolio of pictures about life in Colonial America size 9-1/4" x 12-3/16" has been published for use with this book and other history textbooks. It may be secured from Informative Classroom Picture Publishers, Grand Rapids 2, Michigan. (*Colonial America*—24 plates—$2.95.) Twelve chapters of loose-leaf text are included for reference use by the students.]

Three Levels of Reading Ability

This book is designed for use on three ability levels, to help the teacher provide for the great differences in reading ability found in the average class. It provides a means for purposeful investigation and purposeful reading by students on each of the following ability levels:

1 — A few of the students will read purposefully only the pictures, the map, and many of the captions.

2 — Most of the students will read the pictures and the captions, the map, and much of the text.

3 — Some will read all of the text, the pictures and their captions, and the map.

In each class there will be a few students who will read the book most effectively on the first level only. Each of these students urgently needs a copy of the book for his individual use. The challenging pictures and captions in each chapter make it possible for these students to share many important learning experiences. The teacher will be pleased to observe how much essential information is gained and what thought-provoking experiences are shared by these students, even though they are reading at the first level.

In the average class in which Colonial America is studied, nearly every student will be able to use this book successfully. Each will read at one or more of these ability levels at various times as the study progresses. Students will visit in imagination the early American colonies, and all will gain valuable experiences in history. As a result, all will be able to participate more effectively in group activity, based on an understanding of the important features of life in Colonial America.

How Many Copies Are Needed?

Each teacher must answer the question: "How many copies of this book are needed for my class?" Each teacher must personally assume responsibility for securing the learning aids that will enable his students to learn successfully. If the class is divided into committees, as described on the preceding page, as few as five books and one portfolio can effectively serve a class of thirty students.

The Editors

CONTENTS

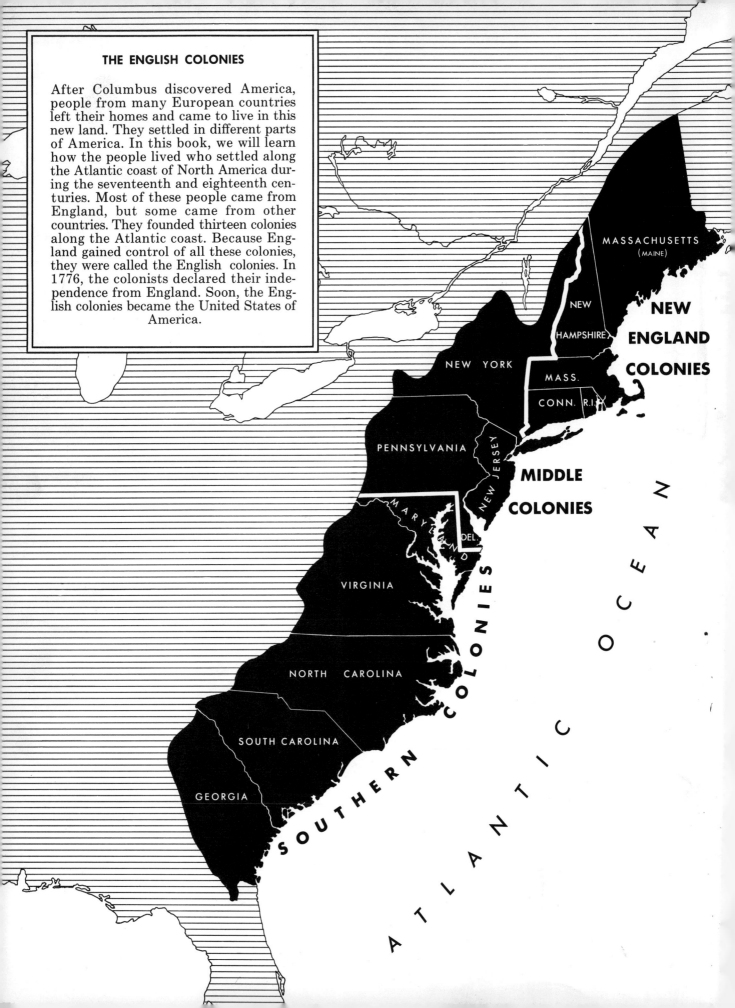

THE ENGLISH COLONIES

After Columbus discovered America, people from many European countries left their homes and came to live in this new land. They settled in different parts of America. In this book, we will learn how the people lived who settled along the Atlantic coast of North America during the seventeenth and eighteenth centuries. Most of these people came from England, but some came from other countries. They founded thirteen colonies along the Atlantic coast. Because England gained control of all these colonies, they were called the English colonies. In 1776, the colonists declared their independence from England. Soon, the English colonies became the United States of America.

MASSACHUSETTS
(MAINE)

NEW
HAMPSHIRE

**NEW
ENGLAND
COLONIES**

NEW YORK

MASS.

CONN. R.I.

PENNSYLVANIA

NEW JERSEY

**MIDDLE
COLONIES**

MARYLAND

DEL.

VIRGINIA

NORTH CAROLINA

S O U T H E R N   C O L O N I E S

SOUTH CAROLINA

GEORGIA

A T L A N T I C   O C E A N

Leaving for a new home. After 1600, many people left England and came to America to live.

CHAPTER ONE

COLONISTS COME TO AMERICA

"The ship is about to sail, Father. Let's go aboard!" said young Miles Griffin impatiently. It was a breezy day in June, 1609, and he was standing on the busy wharf of a port town in England.

The tall man beside him smiled and said, "Give your mother time to say good-by to her friends and relatives, son. She may never see them again. It's hard for her to leave the people she loves and go to a new home in a strange land far away."

Mrs. Griffin gave her sister a last hug. Then she tried hard to smile and said, "I'm ready." Together the family walked up the

* Please see glossary, page 125.   9

Along the Atlantic coast of North America were thirteen
English colonies that later became the United States.
The colonies were divided into three main groups.

Wooden sailing vessels carried the colonists to their new homeland. The voyage took many weeks.

gangplank to the ship. A short time later, the sailors untied the ropes that held the ship to the pier. As they moved slowly out to sea, Miles and the other passengers crowded against the railing to wave good-by to their friends.

"It will be many a day before we see land again," said Mr. Griffin, as the shores of England disappeared from view. "Jamestown, Virginia, is thousands of miles away."

"I hope Virginia is as wonderful as the men of the London Company say it is," said Miles.

"It is," replied his father. "You saw the posters that advertised it. The forests there are full of fur-bearing animals, and there is enough fertile land for everyone to have a good farm. We shall be able to make a much better life for ourselves in America than we ever could in crowded England."

There were times during the long voyage when Miles was afraid the family would never reach their new home. Fierce storms blew the little vessel off course and almost wrecked it. Several passengers became sick with a terrible disease called the plague.* The ship was so crowded and dirty that many others became ill.

One day, after more than two months at sea, Miles and the other passengers saw a faint gray line on the horizon. It was land! The ship sailed slowly into a bay and up a river to Jamestown. Then the sailors dropped the anchor into the water and lowered rowboats over the side of the ship. Miles ducked under the arm of a stout old man and squeezed into one of the boats. Soon he was ashore.

Landing in America. The colonists brought clothes, tools, and other supplies from England.

When he looked about him, Miles could hardly believe his eyes. The people of Jamestown who crowded around the new colonists were as thin and ragged as scarecrows. Their village was just a cluster of tiny huts surrounded by a log fence. The clearing in which it lay hardly made a dent in the dark forest. Miles had never seen a forest as thick as this one. The trees were so tall that they seemed to reach up to the clouds.

Dense forests covered much of the land to which the English colonists came.

Jamestown began as a fort in 1607. It was the first permanent English settlement in America.

Miles couldn't just stand there staring, however, for his father was calling him to help unload their baggage. How glad he was that they had brought food, clothes, and tools with them! They certainly couldn't buy anything they needed here.

When Miles sat down beside his mother to rest a while, she told him how Jamestown had been founded. "A group of men who wanted gold and other riches from America formed the London Company," she explained. "They asked the king of England for land here and for permission to found a colony. Then they put their money together to purchase ships and supplies. Next they found people like us who wanted to come to America. The first group of colonists they sent over arrived two years ago, in 1607. The men of the London Company planned to trade with these people."

13

The Pilgrims,* and some other groups of colonists, came to America to worship God in their own way.

"It doesn't look as though the Jamestown colonists found any gold to send back to the London Company," said Miles as he glanced at the ragged clothes the men were wearing.

"No, it doesn't," agreed Mr. Griffin, who had just joined Miles and his mother. "From the way they look, I think that life here is going to be very difficult at first. But I brought my ax and other tools, and I'm willing to work hard to build a home and clear enough land for a farm. I know you will help me, son."

Miles nodded solemnly. "You can depend on me, Father," he said.

Other English colonies are established. As the years passed, many other colonists came to the Atlantic coast of North America. Like the Griffin family, some came to make a better life. Others came because in their homeland they were not allowed to worship God in the way they thought right. The Pilgrims,* Puritans,* and Quakers* came for this reason.

Altogether, thirteen colonies were established along the Atlantic coast between Florida and Canada. (See map on page 8.) In the north were the New England Colonies of Massachusetts, Connecticut, Rhode Island, and New Hampshire. In the south were Virginia, Maryland, North Carolina, South Carolina, and Georgia. Between the Southern Colonies and those of New England were the Middle Colonies of New York, Pennsylvania, New Jersey, and Delaware.

Not all the people who came to these thirteen colonies along the Atlantic coast of North America were English. Some came

New Amsterdam* was founded by the Dutch in 1626. It was captured by the English and named New York.

from Holland, Sweden, or other countries. However, England was powerful enough to take over the colonies these people started.

From the chapters that follow, you will learn how people in these colonies lived. You will find that they did not always do things the same way in the different colonies. You will also see that colonists during the seventeenth century lived quite differently from the colonists who lived in the eighteenth century. However, you will notice that throughout colonial days people in all the colonies worked hard, and often had good times.

DO YOU KNOW

1. Tell about the experiences you might have had on a ship sailing to America in 1609.
2. With the aid of pictures and the text in this chapter, describe Jamestown.
3. Explain how Jamestown was founded.
4. On the map on page 8, point out the New England, Middle, and Southern Colonies. In which group of colonies was Jamestown?

The first Thanksgiving Day. In 1621, the Pilgrims gathered to thank God for a good harvest.

Bark huts that looked much like Indian lodges were built by some early colonists.

CHAPTER TWO
COLONIAL HOMES

When the early colonists landed in America they had to find shelter quickly. Their first homes were crude dugouts, huts, or cabins. The earliest dugouts were simply caves that the colonists dug into the hillsides. In the South, where the weather was mild, people built huts with thatched roofs. The walls were made of tree branches woven together and plastered with mud. These walls were called "wattle-and-daub." Some northern colonists built shelters that looked much like Indian lodges. Settlers from Sweden built cabins of rough logs. They mixed moss and clay together to fill the narrow cracks between the logs. The roofs were covered with sod or bark. Many of these log cabins had a stone fireplace at one end of the room.

As soon as possible, settlers in all the colonies replaced their crude, temporary shelters with more comfortable houses. Many different kinds of houses were built. Until late in the seventeenth century, most of them were simple in style.

Some colonists built a "common house" in which they lived until their own homes were ready.

Early New England houses were small. Soon, more comfortable houses were built.

Homes in the New England Colonies.   Almost all of the New England colonists used wood in building their permanent homes. To make the framework of a house, large rough logs were hewn into square-shaped timbers. Some of the first houses had thatched roofs like the small English cottages of that time. However, thatch caught fire so easily that these roofs were later replaced with

A two-story house in New England. Many colonists built houses like those they had owned in England.

wooden shingles. The outside walls of the houses were also covered with wooden shingles, or sometimes with boards, to make them warmer and less drafty in winter. These early New England houses had steep roofs, huge chimneys, and small, shuttered windows.

Near the end of the seventeenth century, New England settlers were building two-story homes. The second story often jutted out over the first one, in the style of some English houses of that time. Winding stairways led to the second floors of homes like these.

The Middle Colonies.   People in the Middle Colonies also built houses like those they had left behind in Europe. The Dutch and German colonists often made their homes of brick or stone. Dutch houses were usually two and a half or three and a half stories high and had steep roofs. (See pictures, below and on page 15.) The Germans were the first in the colonies to use stoves rather than fireplaces to heat their homes. Swedish colonists often built sturdy wooden houses with two or three rooms. In such a home, the fireplace was in the corner of the room instead of at the end.

Homes in the Southern Colonies.   Early houses in the Southern Colonies were very much like the small frame cottages built in the north. However, the climate here was mild, and people were not so much concerned about heating their homes. They did not build

A Dutch house built in 1699. In the Middle Colonies, many houses were made of stone and brick.

the chimney of a fireplace inside the house. Instead, it stood against one of the outside walls.

The southern colonists who lived on large farms, called plantations, usually built brick houses. Their homes were a little larger than those of other southern people.

An early southern house. The chimneys of many southern houses were built against the outside walls.

A colonial mansion in the south. By 1750, many wealthy colonists lived in large, beautiful homes.

Eighteenth-century mansions. In the eighteenth century some colonists became wealthy enough to replace their plain, simply made houses with stately mansions. Many of these homes were almost exactly like the houses that were being built by wealthy people in England at that time. They were called "Georgian" houses because they were popular during the years George I, George II, and George III ruled England.

Georgian houses were different from the earlier colonial homes. Windows, doors, and rooms in earlier houses had been placed wherever they seemed to be needed. In most Georgian houses, however, the front door was placed in the center of the house, with exactly the same number of windows on either side of it. Also, their roofs were not so steep as those of earlier houses.

A colonial mansion in New England
This house was built at Cambridge, Massachusetts, in 1759.

A mansion in the Middle Colonies
This house was built in Odessa, Delaware, in 1772.

Mansions like these were first built during the years when George I, George II, and George III ruled England. They are called Georgian houses.

Wealthy colonists used different kinds of materials to build their homes. In New England many Georgian houses were made of wood. Stone was often used in the Middle Colonies, especially in Pennsylvania. Most Georgian houses, however, were built of brick.

In many ways, houses built in the Georgian style were more beautiful than the earlier colonial houses. Slender columns supported the porch roofs of some Georgian houses. The wooden doorframes were often richly decorated with carved designs. These decorations, as well as window frames and doors, were painted a glistening white. Bricks were made in many different colors. The

The Capitol of the Virginia Colony. In this building, the bricks were laid in interesting designs.

Flowers and shrubs were planted to form interesting patterns in the gardens of some eighteenth-century mansions.

bricks of a house might be pink, rose, dark red, purple, or blue-black. Bricklayers often made an interesting design by alternating the long and short sides of the bricks as they built the walls of a house.

Gardens and costly furnishings made Georgian homes seem even more beautiful. The gardens were often as carefully designed as the houses. Footpaths bordered by clipped green hedges wound among beds of bright flowers. The rooms of the houses were usually large, with high ceilings. Soft rugs and graceful, polished furniture added to their beauty.

The architects who designed Georgian houses borrowed many of their ideas about building from the Greeks and Romans who lived many centuries ago. These ancient people erected some of the finest buildings the world has ever seen. They were simple and stately in design, and were often decorated with pillars and fine

Graceful, polished furniture and soft rugs often added beauty to the rooms of Georgian houses.

Jefferson's* house. Colonial architects borrowed ideas about building from the Greeks and Romans.

carvings. Two of the greatest English architects who used these Greek and Roman ideas of building were Sir Christopher Wren and Inigo Jones. Some of the buildings they designed in England in the seventeenth century still stand today.

From English craftsmen, and from books, the colonists learned to construct beautiful Georgian buildings. Some of the carpenters, masons, and other craftsmen who had helped to construct buildings in England came to live in North America. They shared with others their knowledge of designing and building houses and churches like those in their homeland. Books about architecture were sent from England to the colonies. These contained the plans and designs that many wealthy colonists used when they built their homes.

Many homes in the United States today look very much like those the colonists built hundreds of years ago. Some of these are similar to the small, plain houses of early colonial days. Others are like the Georgian homes built in England and in the colonies during the eighteenth century.

─────DO YOU KNOW─────

1. Describe the first shelter you would probably live in, if you were a colonist in early New England.
2. What kinds of colonial houses are mentioned in this chapter? Select pictures that show examples of these houses.
3. Explain how builders in Colonial America learned to construct Georgian houses.

Carved doorways and pillars were among the Greek and Roman decorations used in Georgian buildings.

The warm, cozy kitchen was the most important room in the homes of many colonial families.

CHAPTER THREE
IN AN EARLY COLONIAL KITCHEN

To most colonial families there was perhaps no warmer, more comfortable place in the world than the kitchen. It was the most important room in the house. Sometimes it was the only room. Let us visit a colonial family just as dinner is being prepared in the busy, interesting kitchen of their home.

It is a cold, blustery day. A fire blazes high in the great brick fireplace at one end of the room. The rich odor of venison* stew comes from the bubbling pot hanging from a crane over the fire. Above the hot coals at one side of the fireplace is an iron broiler. Here, three whole rabbits brown slowly.

Our hostess invites us to sit on the settle near the fireplace until dinner is ready. This bench is very narrow and uncomfortable. However, its high, solid back shelters us from the icy drafts that rush in when someone opens the door.

As we look around the kitchen, we see clothes hanging on wooden pegs along the walls. There are no closets. The wooden table, the benches, and the chairs were made by the men in the family. This furniture is heavy and looks uncomfortable.

Muskets* were kept in the kitchen to protect the family against the attacks of unfriendly Indians.

Spinning thread and churning butter were some of the household tasks performed in the kitchen.

A large musket* and a powder horn hang above the fireplace. The musket may be needed to protect the family from attacks by unfriendly Indians. It is also used by the men for hunting deer and other game.

The cow and chickens in the shed behind the house are far too precious to be killed for food. They provide the family with milk and fresh eggs. Also, cream from the cow's milk is churned into butter. Just now Father has set the butter churn near the fireplace. Later, when the cream in the churn has reached the right temperature, one of the children will beat it with the churn's dasher* until yellow flakes of butter appear. Then Mother will wash the butter and mold it into shape.

Now Mother lifts the hinged lid of a large chest in the corner of the room. Much of the family's linen and bedding is stored here. She takes several snow-white linen napkins from it. We shall need them for we will eat most of the dinner with our fingers. The family owns no forks and only a few spoons, made of pewter.*

Long-handled cooking utensils were needed to prepare food in the kitchen fireplace.

On a shelf we see the brass spoon mold in which pewter spoons are made. One of the children tells us how it is used. After the two sides of the mold are clamped together, someone pours melted pewter into the little hole at the bowl end of the mold. The hot liquid inside hardens as it becomes cool. Finally the mold is opened, and out comes a spoon!

A spoon mold was used to make pewter* spoons. Colonists also made spoons of wood and horn.

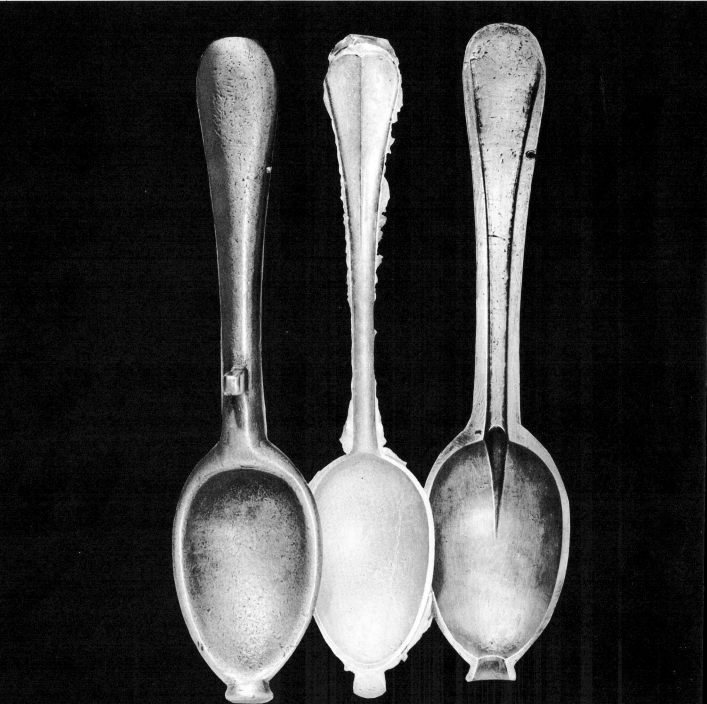

Eating supper in a colonial kitchen. The early colonists did not have forks.

Now the children are setting dishes on the narrow, wooden table. One of them pours warm, frothy milk into the mug set at everyone's place. Mother ladles the hot stew, which she calls "spoon meat," into wooden bowls, or "trenchers." She takes pewter plates from the iron plate warmer near the fireplace. The older girls fill them with pieces of broiled meat and hot corn bread. The corn bread baked all last night in the oven built at one side of the fireplace. This family, like other colonial families, eats corn in some form almost every day in the year.

Wooden Tankard

Pewter Porringers

Pewter Spoon

Trenchers

Dishes and other tableware used by the colonists were usually made of wood or pewter.

Our dessert is a very special treat. The crust of this dried-apple pie was made of expensive white flour stored in a barrel in the shed. Apples for the pie were hung to dry in the loft last fall. Like the other colonists, this family dries many fruits and vegetables for winter use.

When it is time for bed, Mother takes the shiny, brass warming pan from its place near the fireplace and fills it with hot embers. She passes the hot pan between the sheets on the bed. She must move it very fast or it will scorch the sheets.

Father banks the fire carefully, so that it will burn slowly all night. In the morning he will blow the slow fire into flame again with the bellows hanging near the fireplace. If the fire should go out, one of the children will have to go to the neighbor's for hot coals. There are no matches, and it sometimes takes half an hour to light a new fire with flint and tinder.*

We are told that for breakfast tomorrow we shall have waffles and maple syrup. There will also be slices of white bread, which will be toasted in the fire on the iron toasting rack.

─────DO YOU KNOW─────

1. With the help of pictures in this chapter, describe the furniture you would see if you were a guest in a colonial kitchen.
2. What household tasks were carried out in the kitchen of an early colonial home?
3. Look at the pictures on pages 36 and 37. Explain the use of the articles which are mentioned in the text of this chapter.

Kitchen utensils were usually made of iron or copper. They were kept near the fireplace.

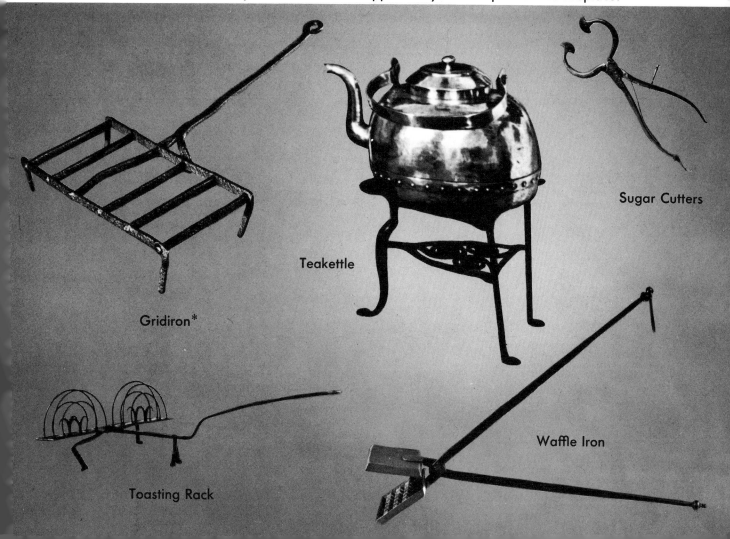

Gridiron*

Teakettle

Sugar Cutters

Toasting Rack

Waffle Iron

Dipping candles. Early colonists made their own candles by dipping wicks into melted tallow.*

CHAPTER FOUR
CANDLES AND LAMPS

Candle-dipping day. What a busy day it was when Mother announced that the time for candlemaking had arrived! First she hung a great iron pot on the crane in the fireplace. Into it went many pounds of beef fat and mutton fat that she had carefully saved for months. Then one of the children sat near the fireplace and swung the kettle slowly over the hot coals.

While the fat was melting into tallow,* many other preparations were made. Mother set two chairs back-to-back at a distance from one another. Across them she laid two poles. The children were kept busy tying wick strings on slender sticks called candle rods. They cut the wick strings twice the length of a candle, twisted them double, and hung them several inches apart on the rods. Finally, Mother lifted the pot of melted tallow from the fire and set it on the floor.

Dip, dip, dip, went each set of wicks into the kettle. A wooden tray lay underneath the poles to catch tallow from the dripping wicks. When the last candle rod was set across the poles, the first wicks were cool enough to be dipped again. Again and again they were dipped, until all the candles were the proper size.

Candleholders were made in different shapes. Those which hung on the wall were called sconces.

Wall Sconce

Wall Sconce

Candleholders

Lantern

The waxy berries of the bayberry bush provided the colonists with wax for fragrant, green candles.

Bayberry candles. In addition to tallow candles, colonists in New England also made very good candles from the wax of bayberries. In September, the bayberry bushes were covered with these grayish-white, waxy berries. The children in a family usually gathered enough berries to make many candles. Then one day in October, all the berries they had picked were boiled in a large kettle of water. As the mixture boiled, the wax in the berries floated to the top and was skimmed off. The skimming went on until there was no wax left in the kettle. Before this wax was used to make candles it was allowed to harden, and then was melted again. Bayberry wax made fragrant, green candles of such fine quality that many of them were sold in England and in other European countries.

Candle molds made candlemaking easier. In later colonial days, people were able to buy metal candle molds that made candle-making simpler and easier. These molds were hollow, tapered tubes and were open at one end. A wick string was placed in each tube. Then, hot wax was poured into them. As the wax cooled, it shrank enough so that the finished candles could be pulled out of the molds without being broken. With candle molds, many candles could be made at the same time.

Making candles in candle molds was easier and faster than dipping them by hand.

Candlelight in late colonial days. As the colonists built larger, finer homes, they used more and more candles. People began to use larger candleholders, called candelabra, which held many candles. In very large homes as many as fifty candles were used in one evening.

In the eighteenth century, colonists began to use candles made from a very unusual kind of wax. This wax was taken from the heads of sperm* whales. Candles made from it burned much more brightly and made less smoke than tallow candles. However, they were very expensive. Only wealthy families could afford them.

In a wealthy colonist's home, candles were sometimes put in chandeliers, which hung from the ceiling.

Putting out a candle. Wealthy families sometimes had special servants to tend the candles.

Such families often had a special servant to tend these expensive candles. During the evening he went from room to room, replacing those that were short or dripping too much wax, and "snuffing" those that were smoking badly. The snuffers worked like a pair of scissors. As the servant snipped the wicks, the burned bits dropped into the little box attached to one blade of the scissors. Snuffing helped to make these expensive candles last longer.

| Betty Lamp | Whale-Oil Lamp | Rush Light |

Colonial lamps. Early colonists used rush lights and Betty lamps. Whale-oil lamps were used later.

Pine torches, or "candlewood." Even the earliest colonists had more light inside their homes than was provided by the bright fires burning in their open fireplaces. They first used torches made from the hearts of pine logs. The resin* in this wood caused it to burn brightly when it was dry. The wood burned with such a clear light that it was named "candlewood." A colonial family often placed one of these lighted torches between two stones in the fireplace. Much of the smoke from the burning torch went up the chimney. Colonists called this means of lighting a room a "candle set."

Rush lights and Betty lamps. Early colonists burned oil and grease in crudely made lamps. One of the most common lamps was a rush light. To make a rush light, part of a dried rush* was soaked with grease and then placed in a holder. These lamps smoked and gave off a bad odor.

The Betty lamp also burned grease. It was shaped like a shallow dish, and was usually made of iron. From its short spout hung a linen wick. This wick absorbed the grease in the dish as it burned.

Whale-oil lamps. In later colonial times, many people used whale-oil lamps. Some were made of glass or pewter* and could be placed on tables or attached to chair backs. Others hung from the wall. Daring seamen often risked their lives hunting whales to provide the oil needed for these lamps.

==DO YOU KNOW==

1. What were some of the ways in which the children in colonial households helped their mothers make candles?
2. Explain how candles were made in molds.
3. Tell about three kinds of candles that were used in America during the colonial period.
4. With the help of the text, tell about the lamps shown in the picture on page 44.

Whalers often risked their lives hunting whales. The colonists used whale oil in their lamps.

A colonial housewife made soap by boiling fat and lye in a big kettle over an open fire.

CHAPTER FIVE
MAKING SOAP

Soapmaking day usually came in the spring. During the long winter months, colonial housewives saved waste grease and bits of fat. When a housewife saw that the yellow bars of hard soap and crocks of soft soap were getting low, she looked at her supply of soap fat. If there was enough, she announced that the first warm spring day would be a good time to make soap.

Before the housewife made her soap, however, she had to prepare another important ingredient. This was lye. First she went to the well and drew up several buckets of water. While the water was getting hot, she placed a wooden barrel on two large wooden blocks in the yard.   Then she put a pail under the small hole in the bottom of this barrel. After filling the barrel with layers of wood ashes and straw, she poured boiling water into it from time to time. The tea-colored liquid that dripped slowly into the pail was lye. It took several days to prepare enough lye for a large supply of soap. Sometimes a container made of rough boards was used instead of a barrel. (See picture on page 48.)

When all the lye was ready, a blazing fire was built underneath the great, black soap kettle. This was also set up outside the house. It hung from a long pole placed across two forked sticks. Into the kettle went the lye and the fat. This mixture had to boil for several hours. Keeping the fire burning, and stirring the thick,

A colonial well. A long pole called a sweep was often used to help raise a bucket of water from a well.

jellylike mass in the kettle was hard work for a colonial house-wife. How glad she must have been to see her crocks filled with soft soap again!

Sometimes the colonists made hard soap. To do this, they added salt to the mixture in the kettle. While the lye and fat were boiling, the part that was soap rose to the top. As this cooled, it hardened. The soap was then taken from the kettle and cut into squares.

─DO YOU KNOW─

1. If you lived in colonial days, what house-hold waste products would your mother save to use in making soap?
2. What important ingredient had to be pre-pared before soapmaking could begin?
3. With the help of pictures in this chapter, explain how colonial housewives made lye and soft soap. How was hard soap made?

Making lye. Colonists made lye by pouring hot water over layers of wood ashes and straw.

Harvesting flax to make linen. Colonists in New England made almost all their own cloth.

CHAPTER SIX
SPINNING AND WEAVING

Women and girls in the New England Colonies spent a great deal of their time spinning thread and weaving cloth. Most people there could not afford to buy clothes sent from England. They raised sheep for wool, and they grew flax for linen. From these materials they made their own sturdy clothing.

Making linen thread.   Flax was usually ready to be harvested and made into linen thread in August. First the graceful plants were pulled up and spread out to dry. Then Father and the boys pulled the seed pods off the flax stalks. This was called "rippling." Next

49

Flax stalks were crushed in a wooden brake to separate the linen fibers from the core and bark.

they tied the stalks into bundles and soaked them in a nearby stream. After soaking, or "retting," for about five days, the flax was taken out, cleaned, and dried.

Now Father and Mother had to separate the linen fibers from the waste material in the stalks of flax. If you look at a stalk of flax, you will see that the linen fibers grow around a hard, woody core. Surrounding them is a tough bark. To get the linen fibers, the flax stalks had to be broken in a heavy wooden "brake." It took a lot of pounding to crush the tough core and bark. Next, the broken bits of core and bark were beaten off the fibers with a heavy "swingling knife." Finally, the fibers were pulled through

50

Removing core and bark from linen fibers was called swingling. The pieces of core and bark were beaten off with a swingling knife.

the teeth of a brush called a "hatchel," to comb out the short and broken fibers. The long flax fibers were spun into linen thread on a spinning wheel.

Mother's flax spinning wheel was quite low, so she sat down to spin. (See picture on page 53.) First she put some flax in the hollow end of a slender stick at one end of the spinning wheel. This stick was called the spindle. It was connected by a belt to a big wheel at the other end of the spinning wheel. Mother made this big wheel turn by stepping on a pedal. As it turned, the spindle also turned, twisting the flax into thread. The thread came out through a hole in the side of the spindle. As Mother guided the fibers into the spindle, she kept dipping her fingers into water, to moisten the flax and keep it from breaking. When her flax

Flax was pulled through a brush called a hatchel to comb out the short and broken fibers.

A spinning wheel was used in many homes to spin flax fibers into strong, linen thread.

was spun into thread, Mother bleached it carefully and put it away to use in weaving.

Making wool thread. Much work was needed to make wool thread. It began when Father and the boys sheared the sheep on a warm day in late spring or early summer. When the shearing was finished, the members of the family carefully removed the burrs and tangled locks from the soft, thick wool. Next the wool was washed. After it was dry, everyone helped to rub it with melted grease.

Now Grandmother brushed the wool between "cards." These looked somewhat like brushes with stiff wire bristles. She laid one card on her knee and placed a little wool on it. Then she stroked the other card across the wool until it was soft and fluffy. As she

Brushing wool between "cards" made it fluffy. Cards looked like brushes with wire teeth.

took the wool off the cards, she made it into a soft roll for Mother to use on the spinning wheel.

Mother had to stand up when she used her wool spinning wheel, because it was so tall. (See picture on page 55.) With her left hand she picked up a little wool and wound it on the end of the spindle. She held on to the wool and gave the big wheel a gentle push with a stick in her right hand. When the spindle began to whir, she pulled the wool out into a long, thin strip, which quickly twisted into thread. As the thread grew longer, she stepped backwards, pulling it out straight. Then she stepped forward to let the new-spun thread wind onto the spindle. It took many turns of the wheel and many steps back and forth before the spindle was full of thread. Now she unwound the thread from the spindle onto a reel. When the reel was full, she slipped off the neatly wound thread.

Before Mother stored away the thread to use in weaving, she dyed it her favorite colors. What hot work it was to stir the brown walnut, or the red pokeberry* dye as it was boiling in the kettle!

Spinning wool. Soft rolls of wool were spun into thread on a tall spinning wheel.

When Mother wanted to dye her thread blue, she dipped it into earthen jars of indigo.*

Weaving.   After Mother had spun enough thread, she wove it into cloth. This was done by hand on a huge, wooden loom. It took a lot of time and patience to get the loom ready for weaving. If you look at a piece of cloth, you will see that some of the threads run up and down, and the other threads run crosswise. (See picture on page 59.) The up-and-down threads are called

Dyeing wool thread. The colonists made dyes from walnuts and berries. They also used indigo.*

Weaving cloth. Cloth was woven on large wooden looms. This homemade cloth was called homespun.

"warp." Mother had to stretch hundreds of these warp threads from the front to the back of her loom. Halfway between the front and back of the loom, she passed them through the "heddles" and the "batten." (See pictures, above and on page 59.)

To understand what heddles are, you must look again at your piece of cloth. You will see that the crosswise threads, called "woof" threads, weave under and over the lengthwise threads. It would have taken Mother much too long to lift each lengthwise thread separately as she wove the crosswise threads through. The heddles did this for her. They were pieces of strong, linen string with little loops, called "eyes," in the middle. The heddles were strung on wooden frames. Each loom had two of these frames. (See picture above.) All the even-numbered, lengthwise threads were put through the loops of the heddles in one frame. The odd-numbered ones were put through the loops in the other frame. By stepping on a pedal at the bottom of the loom, Mother could lift one frame of heddles. This raised half of the lengthwise threads. The threads that passed through the loops of the other frame of heddles remained as they were. Now Mother could easily pass her crosswise thread between the two sets of lengthwise threads. When she did this, she was weaving over and under the lengthwise threads all at once.

If you will look at the pictures on pages 57 and 59, you will see the "batten," which is right in front of the heddles. This is a very heavy wooden frame set with slender strips of reeds. It was banged against the edge of the newly woven cloth to pack the threads close together.

The picture on page 59 also shows you the little boat-shaped "shuttle" in which Mother placed her crosswise thread. It was very smooth and slipped easily between the two sets of lengthwise threads.

When Mother had her loom all ready and her shuttle full of thread, she sat down and began to weave. As she stepped on a pedal, up went one frame of heddles, lifting half the lengthwise threads. Between the two sets of lengthwise threads she passed the shuttle. Then she lowered the set of heddles. Next, she brought the batten forward with a thump, so that its reeds pushed the new crosswise thread into place. Then she pushed down the other pedal, raising the other frame of heddles. Back the other way she passed the shuttle, and then lowered the frame of heddles. Again she pulled the batten forward. This happened over and over, until enough cloth was finished.

Cloth was not yet ready to be made into clothing when it was taken off the loom. Linen material had to be washed and spread out on a clean, grassy field to bleach in the sun. Wool cloth had to be washed and pounded in warm, soapy water. This process, called "fulling," washed out the grease and shrank the material. After the woolen cloth was rinsed, the whole family helped to scratch it with rough thistles called "teasels." "Teaseling" made the material soft and fuzzy. Then, it too was laid out on a grassy field to dry. When we see how much work it took to make cloth in colonial times, we are not surprised that the colonists wore their clothes a long, long time.

─────────────── DO YOU KNOW ───────────────
1. Using the text and pictures of this chapter, explain how housewives in colonial days made linen thread out of flax.
2. Describe the way in which colonial women

made thread out of wool.
3. With the help of the pictures on pages 57 and 59, tell how colonial women wove cloth from the thread they made.

A loom. Lengthwise threads in cloth are called the warp. Crosswise threads are called the woof.

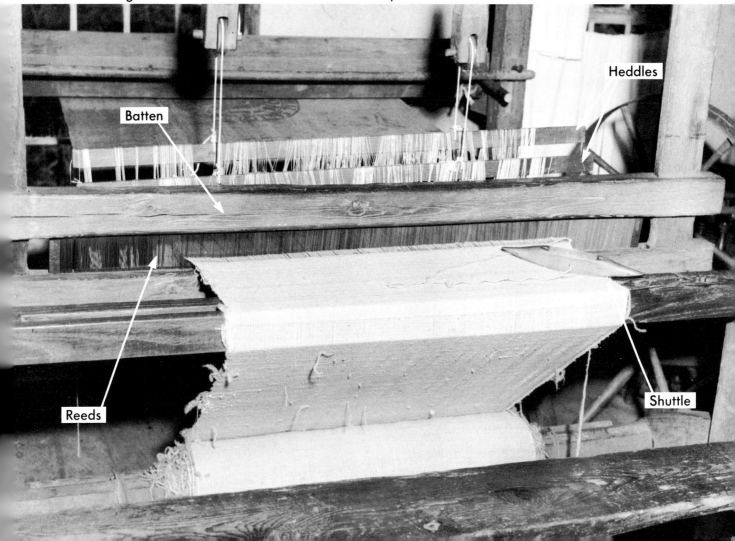

In the New England Colonies, children wore clothes much like those of their parents.

CHAPTER SEVEN
CLOTHING IN COLONIAL TIMES

How neat and prim the little girl looks who welcomes us into her home in New England on this cold, winter day in 1650! Her long-sleeved, gray dress is very plain and simple. The big linen collar she wears is snowy white. So are her cuffs, apron, and little cap. When she introduces us to her mother, we notice that they are both dressed in the same kind of clothes.

The girl's mother asks her to take care of the three-year-old twins. Though one is a girl and the other a boy, they are dressed alike. Both are wearing long dresses, called "petticoats," that have

New England colonists. The Puritans* of New England wore plain, simple clothes.

two pairs of long sleeves. They put their arms through one pair, and the other pair hangs loose at the shoulders. Should the boy go too near the fire, his older sister can grab him by his extra pair of sleeves and pull him back.

Now we hear the father stamping the snow off his feet at the front door. When he comes in he hangs his warm, black cloak and wide-brimmed hat on one of the pegs that have been pounded into the wall. On another peg we see a long, scarlet cloak with a hood, which his wife wears when she rides horseback. Beside it hangs an overskirt, which she puts on over her dress when she goes riding on rainy days. Her husband wears leggings called "spatterdashes" when he rides in the rain.

The father's clothes are also plain. He is wearing long, woolen stockings, and baggy leather breeches. (See picture on page 63.) His black jacket, called a "doublet," is made of two thicknesses of cloth. We notice that the sleeves are not sewed in, but are tied to the armholes of the doublet with pieces of string. Like his wife and daughter, he wears a white collar and white cuffs.

No one in this colonial home wears jewelry, ruffles, or lace. The father explains to us that the Puritan* church to which they belong has made strict rules about the kind of clothes people should wear. Not everyone in New England obeys these rules, but most people do. As time goes on, however, the church will become less strict, and New Englanders will wear brighter, prettier clothing.

Clothing in the Southern Colonies in the seventeenth century. Now let us attend a church service in Virginia to see how people in the Southern Colonies dress. We can tell that there are no strict rules against fancy clothing here. The wealthy men around us are wearing brightly colored breeches and coats of soft velvet or satin. (See picture on page 63.) Their hair curls to their shoulders, and

| Puritans in New England | Quakers* in the Middle Colonies | Wealthy Southern Colonists |

Many kinds of clothing were worn by the colonists during the seventeenth century.

their wide-brimmed hats are decorated with long, flowing plumes. The women's lovely gowns are also made of rich materials, trimmed with lace, ribbons, and ruffles. When they step out into the wind, the ladies cover their faces with silk masks to prevent their skin from becoming rough and chapped. The beautiful clothes these wealthy people wear were sent over from England.

Fancy clothes are not worn all the time in the Southern Colonies. For everyday wear, wealthy colonists have clothing made of plainer materials, such as linen. Poorer people wear clothes very much like those we saw on our visit to New England.

Clothing in the Middle Colonies. Let us now take a stroll through the streets of the busy Dutch settlement of New Amsterdam* on a Sunday afternoon in the seventeenth century. Ahead of us walks a pretty girl wearing several full petticoats. They reach nearly to the ground, but are short enough for us to see her gay, blue stockings and leather shoes. Her loose, full jacket is trimmed with soft fur. A small, closely fitting cap covers her hair. From her belt dangles a bunch of keys, a pair of little scissors, and a pretty pincushion. (See picture below.)

Dutch colonists usually dressed in colorful, loose-fitting clothes. Many children wore wooden shoes.

Buying a hat. In colonial shops, wealthy colonists bought clothes imported from England.

The Dutch men we pass are well dressed. They wear knee-length breeches. Shiny silver buckles ornament their leather shoes, and curling feathers deck their big hats. Some of the men wear a kind of collar, called a "ruff," that is as stiff as a dinner plate.

A man and woman in plainer clothing walk past us now. They are Quakers* from the nearby colony of Pennsylvania. The Quaker church, to which they belong, teaches that people should dress neatly and simply. The woman is wearing a white neckerchief and apron over her gray gown. The man's knee-length breeches and long coat are made of plain, dark-colored material. (See picture on page 63.)

Clothing in the eighteenth century.   Imagine now that a hundred years have passed and we are once more visiting the colonies. We notice that the people in various parts of the country no longer dress so differently from one another. When they go to parties or to church, wealthy men and women in all the colonies dress very much like the planter and his family we shall meet in Chapter Thirteen. (See page 121.) The ladies wear wide hoops to hold out their skirts. The men wear tight, knee-length breeches, long fitted coats, and large cocked hats. Most of the men and boys, and some of the ladies, have wigs on their heads. How uncomfortable these wigs must be!

Wealthy people dressed much alike in all the colonies after 1700. Many men and boys wore wigs.

Working people in Colonial America wore plain clothes. Men often wore leather breeches.

The working people dress in more simple clothing. The women often have white neckerchiefs around their necks. They wear aprons over their long dresses. The men have knee-length breeches and long woolen stockings. Sometimes they wear long-sleeved smocks* instead of shirts or jackets.

──────DO YOU KNOW──────

1. With the help of the picture on page 61, describe the clothing worn by women and girls in early New England.
2. Using the text and picture in this chapter,

tell how the Dutch colonists dressed during the seventeenth century.
3. Describe the clothing worn by colonists during the eighteenth century.

Helping a sick neighbor. Colonists made their own good times by sharing work with friends.

CHAPTER EIGHT
MAKING WORK FUN

The colonists had little time for the kind of fun people enjoy today. They made their own good times while sharing the hard work that was always at hand. Children took part in the work and shared in the fun as well. Sometimes the colonists made a party out of working for a neighbor whose family would be in great distress without their aid. At other times, they helped one another mainly for a chance to share laughter, conversation, and good food.

A "quilting bee."   One of the most tiresome jobs, which colonial women and girls turned into fun, was finishing a new quilt. A housewife first made the patchwork cover for the quilt. Then she made a lining of the same size, usually of plain material but sometimes also of patchwork. Between these two covers she placed an even layer of cotton or wool. Then the four sides of the quilt were attached to the quilting frame with coarse thread or twine. The big frame was then set up like a table top over the backs of four chairs in the front room. Now it was time to invite some of the neighbor women over for a quilting bee.

As many as twelve ladies might sit around the quilting frame, busily sewing the quilt together. With small, even stitches they

A quilting bee. Colonial ladies enjoyed visiting as they helped a neighbor finish a new quilt.

Young girls in colonial times learned to sew and embroider. They tried to make small, even stitches.

followed the design selected by the owner. Little girls often sat nearby, sewing strips of rags together for rugs. One day they, too, would make patchwork quilts and have their own quilting bees.

As their needles flew in and out of the material, the ladies chatted about their families. They discussed other quilts they had made or planned to make later. Colonial women exchanged quilt patterns as women today exchange cooking recipes. The patterns had names such as "Log Cabin," "Job's Trouble," "Rising Sun," or "Sugar Bowl." One patchwork cover might be made of pieces of cotton, wool, and even silk material.

After a quilting bee, a lovely new quilt was ready for someone's bed. The colonial ladies who made it had enjoyed a gay afternoon party.

A sample of fine needlework was called a sampler. Colonial girls showed how well they could sew by embroidering designs with colored silk or yarn.

Kindly words
Will cost but little
Traveling up the hill of life
And they make
The weak and weary
Stronger, braver for the strife

Skating by moonlight. Young people in some colonies went skating on frozen lakes and rivers.

A "feather-stripping" party. The colonists often had a lively party on the evening they stripped the soft down from thousands of goose feathers. When some geese were killed in late summer or fall, the colonial housewife sorted the feathers carefully. She separated the large feathers from the small ones. The small feathers were soft enough to be used as stuffing for new feather beds. The large quills* that had down on them were put into sacks and saved until time for a feather-stripping party that winter. The down would be used as stuffing for soft cushions and quilts.

On the cold, snowy evening of the party, family after family crowded into the warm kitchen. Mothers put their babies to sleep on the wide, feather bed in the bedroom. The older children hurried outdoors to go skating in the moonlight. Later, when they were cold and hungry, they would come in and make popcorn and taffy candy.

Now it was time for the work to begin. All the men and women sat down at a long table in the center of the room. Open pillowcases had been tacked onto the edges of the table. A man and woman sat in front of each of the pillowcases. The women held baskets for the discarded quills on their knees. Then everyone began to strip the down from the feathers as fast as he could. Each person held a feather by its tip with one hand, and with the thumb and forefinger of the other hand he stripped the soft down from the feather. Each couple raced to fill a pillowcase with down before it was time to stop work. The young women stripped the feathers quickly, for their fingers were slender and nimble. Some of the men, however, had big, clumsy fingers that could not move fast. They told funny stories to make up for their slow work. Everyone laughed and talked so much that feather stripping didn't seem to be the hard, messy job it really was.

Later, the feathers and quills were all cleared away. The workers ate a delicious supper of roast goose, cold venison,* hot biscuits, and gingerbread. They drank gallons of cool, sweet cider. Then the older people took the children and babies home. The evening was not yet over for the young people, however. They danced for many hours to the lively tunes of the fiddlers.* At last the young people climbed into their sleighs. They drove swiftly into the night, with moonlight glistening on the snow and sleigh bells echoing their merry laughter.

A house-raising. Neighbors and friends often helped a colonist build his house.

A "house-raising." One of the many jobs a colonist could not do without help was building his house. A man usually put the frame of his house together on the ground and cut the lumber to finish it. Then he invited all the men he knew, and their families, to help him "raise" the house. The women and girls worked hard to prepare enough food for all these hungry men. They set up tables outdoors and piled them high with good things to eat and drink. It took many hours for the group of men and boys to put up the frame of the house. They had to lift and push the side beams of the house into place and lift the heavy rafters for the roof. The colonial family must have been very thankful for their house when the work was finished.

Sugar-making time.   One of the most exciting times of the year for men and boys of the New England Colonies came in late winter or early spring. Soon after the February thaw, they began tramping through the woods to see if the sap was running in the sugar-maple trees. One day they would see a clear liquid on the ends of twigs. This meant that the time for making sugar had arrived. The men then bored small holes in the trunks of the trees and put spouts into them. The boys hung wooden buckets under

Sugar-making time in New England. Colonists boiled sap from maple trees to make syrup or sugar.

these spouts to catch the running sap. Everyone helped to set up the big sugaring-off kettles and to build roaring fires under them. The sap that collected in the buckets was boiled into clear, sweet maple syrup or, by boiling it longer, into maple sugar.

Sometimes the men and boys worked at the sugar camp for several days. At night they sat near a warm campfire, watching the stars shining through the dark trees. It was so quiet they could hear the drip, drip, drip of the running sap.

Often, there was a party on the last day at the camp. People from nearby farms came by sled to the maple grove. Everyone

A sugar-making camp. The sweet smell of boiling syrup sometimes attracted wild animals.

A cornhusking bee. Neighbors in colonial times made a party of husking and shelling corn.

tasted the new maple sugar many times. Now and then, the men poured some of the warm syrup on the snow to make maple-sugar candy for the children.

In many other ways, the colonists turned their hard work into good times. They made parties of husking and shelling bushels of corn. They had plowing bees and house-cleaning bees. To these sturdy, courageous people, "neighborliness" was next to "godliness," and almost any kind of neighborliness was fun.

---DO YOU KNOW---

1. Describe a "quilting bee" and a "house-raising." Why do you suppose the early colonists held parties such as these?
2. Select pictures in this chapter that show how families in Colonial America had good times by sharing hard work.
3. Explain how the men and boys in colonial New England made maple syrup and sugar.

A "dame school." In early New England, children were often taught by a housewife in her home.

CHAPTER NINE
COLONIAL SCHOOLS

In very early colonial days, children could not go to school as they do today. There were no schoolhouses, no teachers, and only a few books. Boys and girls had to learn what they could from their parents at home. However, some parents could not read or write.

Education in New England. The first schools in New England were called "dame schools." Housewives were the teachers and their homes were the schools. They gathered the neighborhood children around their fireplaces and taught them to read, write, and spell. These housewives were not expected to neglect their own work while they were teaching. Often they went busily on with their spinning, weaving, or knitting, while the students recited their lessons.

Sometimes the only books the students had were hornbooks. These were not real books. Usually they were flat, wooden boards shaped like paddles. A piece of paper, with the alphabet and the Lord's Prayer printed on it, was tacked to the board and covered with a thin sheet of transparent horn. (See picture below.)

In 1647, public schools were started in New England. A law was passed which required every town of fifty or more families to establish a grade school. Towns with one hundred or more families had to start a high school as well.

A hornbook and a "New England Primer" were used by school children in the New England Colonies.

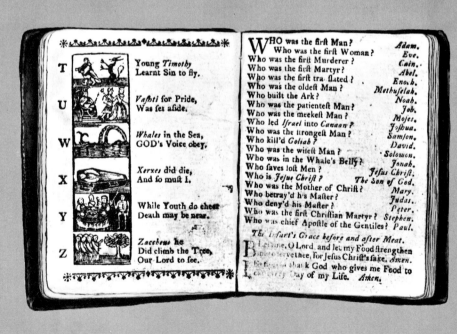

Hornbook

New England Primer

A New England schoolroom was gloomy and uncomfortable. The teacher was often very strict.

A visit to a New England public grade school.   Imagine that it is a winter morning in 1750 and you are on your way to visit a public grade school in colonial New England. The little log schoolhouse stands in a clearing at one end of the town. As you enter the schoolroom, you see that some of the children are sitting on wooden benches. They are studying together quietly. The others are standing by the wall, reciting their lessons to the schoolmaster. Today, they are learning a prayer from a book called the *New England Primer*. The primer also contains spelling words, short poems, questions about the Bible, and the alphabet. This book and the Bible are the only textbooks these children use.

When you look around the schoolroom, you see that there are no blackboards, maps, or pictures on the wall. The room is very gloomy except for the blazing fire in the huge fireplace at one end. All the students must bring wood for the fireplace. Anyone who fails to bring his share has to sit in a corner, far away from the warmth of the fire.

School is not much fun for these children. The teacher is very strict and does not hesitate to whip them when they misbehave or make mistakes. Saturday is not a holiday, so they must attend school six days a week. Classes begin at seven or eight in the morning and do not end until four or five o'clock in the afternoon.

None of the girls you see here will go on to high school, but a few of the boys will. They will attend a Latin grammar school, where most of their time will be spent studying the Latin language.

Education in the Middle Colonies. Like the New England colonists, people in the Middle Colonies established schools as soon as possible. In the Dutch colony of New Netherland,* each church had its own school. The government paid a large part of the cost of running these schools, and the parents who were able to do so paid a small fee. Most of the boys and girls attended school. When the English took over this colony, however, the government stopped most of its help to the schools.

Education in the Southern Colonies. Almost no schools were established in the Southern Colonies. It was difficult to start schools there, for people lived on widely separated farms. Also, many southern colonists did not think that learning was important. Wealthy planters who wanted to educate their children hired private teachers from England, but nobody bothered to teach the boys and girls from poor families.

Colleges in the colonies. Only young men went to college in colonial times. Wealthy colonists in the south usually sent their sons to universities in England. There were also nine colleges in the colonies. Most of these were started by churches to train young men to become ministers. Some of these early colleges have become great universities.

---DO YOU KNOW---

1. With the help of the picture on page 78, describe a New England "dame" school.
2. Compare your classroom with the colonial schoolroom shown on page 80.
3. How were schools supported in the Dutch colony of New Netherland?
4. Why were few schools established in the Southern Colonies?

Dartmouth College was founded in 1769. Students were called to class with a conch shell.

Before a church was built, some New England colonists worshiped together under the trees.

CHAPTER TEN
THE CHURCH IN NEW ENGLAND

Many of the New England colonists came to America to gain religious freedom. One of the first buildings in almost every new settlement was a church, or meetinghouse. Until they could build a meetinghouse, these brave people sometimes held church services under the trees.

An early New England meetinghouse. The first churches in New England were plain, wooden buildings.

In the early days of the colonies, the meetinghouse was a plain, unpainted wooden building. Sometimes it had a bell tower in the center of the roof. Often the meetinghouse was used as a fort also. The early colonists never felt free from the danger of Indian attacks. They kept their guns beside them, even when they went to church.

As time went on, the New England colonists built larger and more elaborate churches. These were painted white, and had tall bell towers with graceful spires rising from them.

84

A later New England church. Later churches were painted white and usually had bell towers, topped with slender spires.

On Sunday, New England colonists prayed, read the Bible, and attended long church services.

Everyone in the New England Colonies had to attend church on Sunday. Extreme illness was the only excuse for staying home. There were church services in the morning as well as in the afternoon. People who lived far from town brought their lunches, or cooked a hot meal in the "Sabbath house," which was next to the church.

The meetinghouse was cold and uncomfortable in the winter, for it was never heated. To deliver his sermon, the minister stood in a pulpit high above the pews. He sometimes talked for five hours. Members of the congregation sat stiffly in straight-backed wooden pews, with their feet resting on foot warmers they had brought from home. (See picture below.) These were little metal boxes filled with hot coals from the fireplaces. Though they stayed warm for a while, the hot coals in them burned out long before the end of such a long sermon.

In some churches a tithingman kept people awake during the long service. This man walked up and down the aisles, carrying a long rod. Feathers were attached to one end of the rod and a knob

In church, the colonists kept their feet warm on little metal boxes that were filled with hot coals.

The tithingman tickled sleepy people with feathers to keep them awake during church services.

to the other end. If anyone nodded or dozed a bit, he was tickled with the feathers. However, if a person fell fast asleep, he was whacked soundly with the knob.

Throughout colonial days, the meetinghouse was far more than a church to the people of New England. Men gathered there for public meetings, or just to hear the news. The meetinghouse nearly always stood in the center of town, where everyone could reach it easily.

One group of colonists who came to New England for religious freedom thought that everyone should worship in the same way they did. These people were the Puritans,* who came from England. There were so many Puritans that they were able to control the government in much of New England. Only Puritans were allowed to vote. Every person was expected to obey the strict laws

A public meeting in church. In New England, public meetings were often held in the churches.

People who broke the law were often punished by being locked in the stocks for many hours.

made by the Puritans, even if he did not belong to their church. People who broke these laws were punished, and sometimes even lost their church membership. When this happened, they could no longer vote.

Punishment for lawbreakers was often severe and cruel in colonial days. If a person told a lie, he could be made to sit for many hours with his feet fastened securely in stocks. (See picture above.) Or, he might have to stand on a platform with his head and hands locked in a pillory.* For other minor offenses, a man might be tied to a whipping post and given several lashes with a whip. The stocks and pillory usually stood near the village meetinghouse. Here, other colonists would gather to jeer at the prisoner. Many people believed that a person who could be made to feel ashamed would be careful not to break the law again.

A gossipy woman or one who nagged her husband was sometimes punished by means of a "ducking stool." The guilty person was tied in a chair at one end of a wooden pole that extended over a pond. Several strong men moved the other end of the pole up and down, ducking the woman into the cold water. The laughs of onlookers would often hurt more than the ducking.

---DO YOU KNOW---
1. What were colonial meetinghouses used for, besides church services?
2. Tell how you might have spent a winter Sunday, if your family had lived in New England during colonial days.
3. Describe some of the ways in which law-breakers were punished in the New England Colonies. What was a pillory?

A gossipy woman was sometimes tied in a chair at the end of a long pole and ducked in a pond.

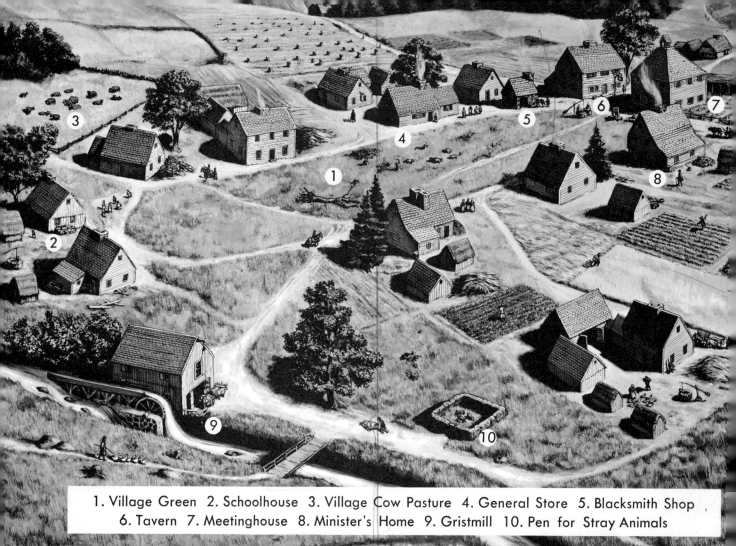

1. Village Green 2. Schoolhouse 3. Village Cow Pasture 4. General Store 5. Blacksmith Shop
6. Tavern 7. Meetinghouse 8. Minister's Home 9. Gristmill 10. Pen for Stray Animals

A New England village in 1700. Many people in the New England Colonies lived in small villages.

CHAPTER ELEVEN
A NEW ENGLAND VILLAGE

There were many villages in the New England Colonies. Farmers here grouped their farms around small communities instead of living far apart, as farmers in the Southern Colonies did. Let us visit one of these early farming villages and see what it is like.

The horses we are riding kick up a cloud of dust as they trot down the dirt road to the village. Far ahead of us we see a church and a small cluster of shops and houses. This is the center of the village. Farmhouses are built around it in all directions. We wave good morning to a little girl standing in the doorway of one home.

We are riding into the village now. The houses are quite far apart. Close by each house are several small sheds and a barn. Some of the barns are connected to the houses with closed passageways. The people who live in these homes will not have to walk through the snow when they feed their farm animals in winter. (See picture on page 92.) In many of the yards, we see stacks of firewood.

The street along which we are riding leads to an open, grassy space in the middle of the village. This is called the "green." When the village was very small, all the families used the green as a pasture for their cows. The first villagers built their homes around this pasture. On one side they built the church, or meetinghouse. As the village grew larger, more houses were built behind the first ones. Streets were made between these houses. By that time there were too many cows to graze on the green, so another pasture was chosen outside the village. Now the green is just a pleasant, grassy space in the center of town. Children often play games here.

Several horses are waiting in the horse sheds behind the meetinghouse, so we know a meeting must be going on. Since it is Thursday morning, we know it is not a church service. We enter the meetinghouse and ask a man what the people are doing here. He says they·are having a town meeting. Once or twice a year, all the men from the village and the surrounding farms come here for a meeting like this. They vote for the men who will govern the village for the next year. They also elect a policeman and other community helpers. At these meetings, the men talk about the problems of the village. Just now they are discussing how much

Delivering mail. Postriders on horseback carried mail from town to town.

they should pay the schoolmaster. Some of the men think they should raise his salary. They decide to vote on it. We notice that some of the men do not vote. The man next to us explains that they are not allowed to vote, because they are not church members or do not own land.

When the town meeting is over, we follow the men out of the church. Several of them walk over to see a man who is being punished for telling a lie. He is sitting on a wooden platform in front of the church. His legs are stretched out straight before him, and his feet are locked into the holes of a wooden frame called the stocks. The men tell us that this kind of punishment is common in the colonies.

We walk away and join the group of men who are going next door to the White Stag Tavern for a mug of cider. The tavern is a two-storied building with a sign in front, showing the picture of a white stag.* Inside are wooden chairs, tables, and a large fireplace. The villagers and the men from nearby farms often gather here to visit. Mail is delivered here by the postrider, who goes from town to town on horseback. Several of the men look through the letters on a table near the wall to see if they have received any mail.

Some travelers are staying at the White Stag Tavern. We talk to a man who is on his way to the city of Boston. He has come from a port town on the coast. The traveler tells us that there are

A village near the sea. There were many port towns and fishing villages on the coast of New England.

good harbors along the rugged New England coast, and many port towns have been built there.

The traveler has a copy of a Boston newspaper called the *News-Letter*. In it we find news from England as well as stories about things that have happened in the colonies. The traveler tells us that there are not many newspapers in the colonies. Instead, most villagers hear the news from a town crier. This is a man who walks through the streets ringing a bell to get people's attention. As they gather about him, he shouts the important news. (See picture on opposite page.)

It is getting dark now, and the men begin to go home for supper. After the tavernkeeper serves us our meal, we go upstairs

Reading the newspaper. By 1775, over thirty different newspapers were published in the colonies.

to bed. We are surprised to learn that we must share our room with some travelers we never met before.

We lie very close to the edge of the bed so that we can look out the window. One by one the lights in the houses are going out. There are no street lights, so the streets are very dark. The only light we see is from a lantern carried by the night watchman. As he passes the White Stag, he calls out, "Ten o'clock and all is well." When he turns the corner, the street is dark again, and everything is very, very quiet.

DO YOU KNOW

1. Look at the picture on page 92. Where is the village "green"? How was this space used when the village was first settled?
2. Tell three ways in which the people living

in a colonial village might receive news.
3. With the help of the picture on page 95, describe what you might see if you visited an early New England village near the sea.

The night watchman carried a lantern through the streets at night and called out the time.

Plowing a field. Farming was the most important way of earning a living in Colonial America.

CHAPTER TWELVE
EARNING A LIVING

Throughout colonial times, most of the people made their living by farming. At first, almost all the colonists were farmers. Dense forests covered the land to which these early people came. If there was to be enough food to eat, nearly everyone had to help clear the fields and plant and harvest the crops. There was no farm machinery, so all this work had to be done by hand. Farmers used oxen or horses to pull their heavy plows. They cut their grain with scythes* or sickles.* With these simple farming methods,

Shipbuilders made sturdy sailing vessels, which the colonists used for fishing, whaling, and trading.

one man could not produce much food. When the early colonial farmers needed shoes, furniture, or other articles, they had to make them at home in their spare time.

As time went on, and more and more land was cleared, it became easier to raise food. Many farm workers were still needed, of course, but some men were able to earn their living in other ways.

Fishermen, sailors, and merchants. In New England, some men earned their living from the sea. There were several reasons for this. Farming in New England was difficult, for the soil was thin and rocky and the winters were very long. However, the ocean nearby was full of fish, and there were many good harbors along the coast. Fishing soon became a very important way of earning a living in New England. Fishermen caught more fish than they needed, so they cleaned and dried them to keep them from spoiling. Then they shipped them to markets in Europe. There the dried fish were exchanged for cloth and other manufactured goods the colonists needed. Many men worked as sailors on the ships that carried goods back and forth from Europe. Some colonists became merchants and sold the goods that were brought back to the colonies.

Other men earned their living by hunting whales. While they were at sea, they cut up the whales they killed. Then they boiled the blubber, or whale fat, to obtain whale oil. This oil was used in lamps to light the homes of the colonists.

Shipbuilders and lumbermen. The sailors, fishermen, and whalers needed sturdy ships, and many men worked to provide them.

Lumbermen cut trees for wood needed in building ships. The colonists also sold lumber to England.

Some men cut trees for the wood that was used in building ships. Others worked as shipbuilders. Colonial boys in many coastal towns enjoyed watching these skilled workers fit boards tightly together to make the hulls and decks of sailing vessels. They also watched the men who cut and stitched heavy canvas to make the billowing white sails.

New England lumbermen and shipbuilders cut more lumber and made more ships than the colonists needed. They sold these to people in other countries.

Coopers. Some men in seaside towns earned their living by making barrels. These men were called coopers. The barrels they made were used to store and to ship such goods as fish, rum, molasses, and whale oil. It took great skill to fit the wooden barrel staves together and fasten them tightly with strong hoops of wood.

Coopers were skilled workers who made wooden barrels in which goods were stored and shipped.

Chairs, tables, benches, and other wooden articles were made by colonial cabinetmakers.

Cabinetmakers. Among the other men who earned their living by making wooden articles were cabinetmakers. With their simple hand tools, they made tables, chairs, chests, and beds for colonial families who could afford to buy them. They also fashioned beautiful wooden panels to cover the rough walls in some colonial homes.

The blacksmith made iron horseshoes, tools, kettles, and many other useful articles.

The blacksmith.   The village blacksmith also made many articles which the colonists used. Colonial children loved to gather at the door of his smoky shop to watch him pound pieces of glowing iron into horseshoes, oxshoes, hinges, tools, and nails. Once in a while the children saw him use his iron pincers to pull out someone's aching tooth. There were no dentists in colonial days.

The miller. Often, colonial boys and girls carried the family's corn to the gristmill. This was usually built by a rushing stream or waterfall. Running water turned the huge, wooden wheel that made the heavy millstone turn round. The miller used this millstone to crush hard kernels of corn into fine meal.

A gristmill. The mill's water wheel turned a heavy stone which crushed kernels of corn into meal.

Shoemakers in the colonies made shoes by hand. Colonial shoes could be worn on either foot.

The shoemaker.   The village shoemaker was another important workman in colonial times. He cut and sewed shoes and boots by hand, and fastened the heels on with wooden pegs. The shoes he made could be worn on either foot. Sometimes the shoemaker carried his tools with him and traveled from farm to farm, making shoes for people in the country. Since most people in Colonial America had to walk every place they went, the shoemaker spent a great deal of his time mending worn shoes.

The traveling shoemaker carried his tools with him. He went from farm to farm, making shoes for people in the country.

Printing a newspaper. Colonial newspapers printed news about England as well as the colonies.

Other trades.   There were many other ways of earning a living in Colonial America. The dyer and his helpers stirred the housewife's homespun cloth in great vats of steaming-hot dye. Few people liked to go near the dyehouse because of its bad smells. The wigmaker made elegant wigs for colonial gentlemen. Sometimes he fashioned expensive wigs from human hair. Less costly ones were made of horsehair, goat hair, or silk thread. The printer published the colony's newspaper in his cluttered shop. The

The wigmaker made many different kinds of wigs for colonial gentlemen. Some wigs were made of horsehair and others were made of thread.

spoon maker melted down old, battered pewter spoons and made new ones. Leaky pots and pans were mended by the traveling tinsmith, or "tinker." Sometimes these tradesmen were not paid with money. Instead, the colonial housewife agreed to give them food or household goods in return for their services.

─────DO YOU KNOW─────

1. Why was fishing an important way of earning a living in the New England Colonies?
2. Select pictures in this chapter that show wood products made by the colonists.
3. What are some of the articles you might find in a colonial blacksmith's shop?
4. Describe some of the ways in which a man could earn a living in Colonial America.

Weighing silver. Colonial silversmiths sometimes made beautiful silverware from silver coins.

Tobacco, rice, and other crops were grown in the Southern Colonies on large farms called plantations.

CHAPTER THIRTEEN
LIFE ON A SOUTHERN PLANTATION

In the Southern Colonies the soil was rich and summer days were very hot. Tobacco, rice, indigo,* and cotton grew well there. Because people in England were willing to pay good prices for these products, some southern colonists became very wealthy. Often these men owned farms that were too large for them to work by themselves. They bought Negro slaves to plant and harvest their crops. Their large, slave-worked farms were called plantations. As time went on, many plantation owners built beautiful homes, where they lived in comfort and leisure. Come with us as we pay a visit to a large rice plantation in the colony of South Carolina.

The plantation owner's home.   It is a fine summer day in 1760. Our horse-drawn carriage wheels briskly up the driveway that curves from the plantation gates to the steps of the planter's stately home. We stop before a house that is two stories high and made of rose-colored brick. High, wide chimneys are built at either end of the house. The window frames and doorway gleam with fresh, white paint. This house looks very much like the home of a rich landowner in England.

Arriving by horse-drawn carriage. Plantations in the Southern Colonies were usually far apart.

The kitchen of a plantation home was often located in a small building apart from the house.

A Negro butler meets us at the door. He leads us through the great central hall and past the wide staircase to the parlor. High ceilings and large windows help make these rooms cool and airy even in this hot climate. All around us we see polished furniture, fine carpets, brocade* curtains, and delicate ornaments that were imported from England. There is no kitchen in this beautiful home. Meals are prepared in a separate kitchen house. In this way, the family is not bothered by the heat of the cook's fire or the smell of food that is being prepared.

Slaves and their mistress. Negro slaves did almost all the work on a southern plantation.

The plantation owner's wife welcomes us into the parlor. It is early in the day, and she is still wearing an everyday dress of dark-colored material. Although the planter's wife does not do any housework, she keeps very busy supervising the many Negro slaves who take care of the large house. Now she must go to a slave cabin to see a sick baby. There is no doctor on the plantation, so the mistress of the house helps the people who are sick.

Before she leaves, our hostess asks us if we would like to go into the music room and listen to her daughter play the harpsichord. The small, lovely, music room opens directly off the parlor. Here we see a graceful, golden harp and a flute, as well as the harpsichord. The harpsichord is a stringed instrument that looks somewhat like a piano. It is decorated with dainty carvings and paintings. The planter's daughter, like most other wealthy colonial girls, has taken music lessons ever since she was very small. Her flying fingers bring delicate, sweet music from the instrument.

When she has finished playing, the planter's daughter takes us to the schoolroom. Here, her two younger brothers and the children from several nearby plantations are studying their

Playing the harpsichord. Many southern girls from wealthy families studied music.

lessons. Because most of the plantations in this region are so far apart, there is no regular school here. Our host and his closest neighbors had to hire a teacher from England to instruct their children at home. When the boys are older they will either go to William and Mary College in Williamsburg, Virginia, or finish their studies in England.

Suddenly we hear horses' hoofs on the driveway. We walk to the front door as the planter and his overseer dismount at the front steps. The overseer is a white man hired by the planter to supervise the field slaves. The two men talk about a shipment of rice that must go out this morning. Then the overseer mounts his horse and rides to his small house nearby. The planter greets us very graciously and asks us if we would like to tour his plantation.

A plantation schoolroom. Planters hired private teachers from England to teach their children.

A plantation. Behind the owner's house were slave cabins, orchards, barns, and fields.

A tour through a southern plantation.   As we wait for the stableboy to bring riding horses, we look over the rolling green lawn that stretches to the river's edge. Sheep are grazing on the lower slope. The planter does not have a lawn mower, but these sheep keep his grass short. Near the house we see a lovely garden. Little footpaths wind among the beautifully shaped flower beds.

A Negro boy helps us mount our horses, and we ride to the back of the house. Here we see the cabins of the house slaves. Nearby are the stables, the orchard, and the kitchen gardens, where vegetables for the family are grown. We pass the spinning and weaving houses, where cloth for household uses and for the slaves' clothing is made. A little farther on we see the carpenter's

A rice field. The planter provided his slaves with a home, food, and clothing, but he paid them no wages.

and shoemaker's shops and a smoky shed where the plantation blacksmith does his work. The plantation is so far from any town that almost everything the people need must be made right here. Some of the workers we see are white, indentured servants. These people were unable to pay their own boat fare from England to America. They agreed to work for the plantation owner without wages for four years if he would pay for their passage.

Soon we come to the rice fields. Acres of bright-green plants stretch as far as we can see. Dozens of Negro slaves dressed in blue linen clothing are busy weeding the marshy fields.

Now we ride down to the plantation wharf. A small sailing ship is being loaded with rice for markets in England. While we are here, the anchor is raised and the ship sails slowly down the river toward the Atlantic Ocean. Most of the southern plantations are near rivers, because the cheapest and most convenient way to transport goods in Colonial America is by water.

When we return to the big house, the planter's wife joins us on the porch. Some friends from neighboring plantations are coming over for supper and an evening of dancing, and she asks us if we will be able to stay. When we accept her invitation, she calls a maid to show us upstairs to a guest room. Here we rest and

A guest room. Carved furniture and costly rugs helped to make the planter's home beautiful.

change our clothes. The guest room has a large four-poster bed with flowered bed curtains. At the windows hang long curtains made of brocade. Cushioned chairs, bright carpets, and pictures make the room comfortable and lovely. The maid pours water from a white pitcher into a large basin on a washstand in the corner. There is no running water in this colonial home.

We hear the planter's children come upstairs with their Negro mammy. She is a friendly, motherly looking woman who has taken care of them since they were born. Right now, she is scolding one

A child's room. The planter's children were usually cared for by a Negro servant.

of the boys for tearing his coat. However, we can tell by the way the children laugh and tease that they love her very much.

Good times on a southern plantation.   People on a southern plantation must make their own good times. More than anything else, they enjoy visiting with their friends. Because plantations are so far apart, it often takes a long time to reach a neighbor's house. When people visit, they usually stay overnight or longer.

Below us, we hear the planter's wife directing the slaves as they prepare the house for tonight's guests. Extra beds are set up in all the guest rooms. The gardeners bring in great armloads of flowers. From our window, we watch a Negro boy as he polishes a large silver platter. When we come downstairs, we see tall, slender candles glowing in dozens of silver candleholders. The parlor rugs have been taken up, and the floor gleams like a dark mirror.

The planter and his family are dressed in their best clothes. Both the mistress and her daughter wear gowns of rich brocade with hooped skirts and satin petticoats. Their elbow-length sleeves and tight bodices are bordered with ruffles of delicate lace. Snowy white powder has been sprinkled over their carefully curled hair. The planter wears a knee-length coat made of blue brocade and lined with velvet. His black satin trousers are fastened at the knee with silver buckles. Frills of lace show beneath his cuffs and at the neck of his embroidered waistcoat. He also wears long, white stockings and red leather shoes. On his head he wears a heavy, white wig. The two little boys are dressed just as he is, even to the wig.

Now the guests begin to arrive. Stableboys wait at the front steps to lead their horses and carriages around to the coach yard. Soon the house is filled with talk, laughter, and music. The beautifully dressed ladies and gentlemen choose their partners for the

The graceful minuet was one of the favorite dances enjoyed by colonists at parties.

first dance. It is a minuet, which is one of the favorite dances in Europe at this time. The ladies' full skirts swirl and sway as they step through the slow, graceful movements of the dance. At nine o'clock, the doors of the dining room are thrown open. On the long, mahogany table, there are glowing candles and platters filled with delicious food. After supper most of the guests return to

A small dinner party. Southern colonists liked to visit their friends. Guests sometimes stayed for a week or longer.

their dancing. Some of the older people go into the library to play cards. A group of younger men gathers by the window to talk about tomorrow's hunt.

We step outside onto the wide back porch to catch a breath of fresh air. Far across the fields we hear the sound of singing. The slaves have built a huge bonfire near their cabins. We walk down to the edge of the fence and watch them sing and dance in the firelight.

─────────────────────DO YOU KNOW─────────────────────

1. Using the pictures and text of this chapter, describe a southern plantation.
2. What crops were grown on plantations? Why were fields often located near rivers?
3. With the help of pictures in this chapter, describe the home of a plantation owner.
4. Tell about the work done by the house slaves and the field slaves on a plantation.

After the day's work was over, the slaves sometimes sang and danced by the light of a fire.

GLOSSARY

Your study of Colonial America will be more interesting if you take time to use this glossary. You should turn to this glossary each time a word that you read in the text is marked with an asterisk (*), unless you clearly understand the word. The meaning of each word in the glossary is explained to help you understand the text and pictures in this book. You will learn much more about Colonial America if you will use this glossary.

brocade. Cloth with a raised design woven into it, usually with silk, silver, or gold thread.

dasher. A long, wooden rod with crossed pieces of wood fastened to the lower end. Used to stir cream in a churn. The dasher was plunged up and down in the churn until the cream separated into butter and buttermilk.

fiddlers. Another name for violin players.

indigo. Certain plants of the pea family and the mustard family which yield a blue dye. From this plant, colonists obtained a deep-blue dye which they used to color cloth.

Jefferson, Thomas, 1743-1826. The third president of the United States. Jefferson also was a fine architect. He used Roman ideas in designing Monticello, his home in Virginia. (See picture, page 28.)

musket. A gun used by soldiers and hunters until the rifle came into general use. The barrel of a musket was smooth inside, like the barrel of a shotgun.

New Amsterdam. The former name of New York City. New Amsterdam was founded by Dutch colonists in 1625. In 1664, the city was captured by the English and renamed New York.

New Netherland. A colony founded in 1624 by Dutch settlers. It was located along the Hudson and Delaware rivers. This colony was captured by the English in 1664. See **New Amsterdam.**

pewter. Pewter is made by combining tin and one or more other metals, such as lead or copper. Used by American colonists to make tableware.

Pilgrims. The people who founded Plymouth Colony in Massachusetts. The Pilgrims belonged to an English religious group which had separated from the Church of England. In 1620, the Pilgrims sailed to America in the "Mayflower" to seek religious freedom.

pillory. A colonial instrument of punishment for persons guilty of minor offenses. The pillory was made of wooden boards with holes cut in them, and was usually located in the town square. As the prisoner stood behind the pillory, his head and arms were put through the holes and locked in place. Colonists laughed at the prisoner and often threw things at him.

plague. Any disease that is dangerous and which spreads easily from one person to another.

pokeberry dye. A red dye made from the juicy, dark-purple berries of the pokeweed plant.

Puritans. Persons who belonged to any one of several Protestant groups in England and in New England. The Puritans believed in a simple form of worship and a simple method of church organization.

Quakers. Members of a religious group, called the Society of Friends, organized in England by George Fox about 1650. The colony of Pennsylvania was founded by William Penn, leader of a group of Quakers who had come to America to find religious freedom.

quill. The stiff, horny part of a feather. Also, one of the tail or wing feathers of a bird. Sharpened goose quills were used for writing before metal-pointed pens were invented.

resin. A substance found in certain plants and trees, especially pines and firs. Resin is yellow, brown, or almost black in color.

rush. A grasslike, hollow-stemmed plant which grows in swamp areas. Rush stems are sometimes used in making mats and chair seats.

scythe. A farm tool used for mowing hay crops or grain by hand. The scythe has a long wooden handle with a curved cutting blade attached to one end. To cut hay or grain, the reaper grasps the handle with both hands and swings the scythe in front of him from right to left.

sickle. A farm tool used for cutting hay crops or grain. A sickle has a short wooden handle, with a sharp, curved blade attached to one end. Colonists used sickles to harvest hay or grain in fields where there were too many tree stumps to allow use of scythes. See **scythe.**

smock. A light, loose garment worn over other clothes to protect them from dirt or stains.

sperm whale. A kind of whale found in warm ocean waters. Colonial whalers hunted this whale to obtain wax and oil. These were found in a large space in the whale's skull, and also in the fat of the whale.

stag. A full-grown, male red deer. Also called a hart. Found in certain parts of Europe and Asia.

tallow. Animal fat, especially of cattle and sheep. Pure tallow is obtained from the fat by a melting process. The colonists used tallow in making soap and candles.

tinder. A dry substance, such as scorched linen, that will easily catch fire from a spark. The colonists usually kept tinder, steel, and flint in a tinder box. They made sparks by striking the flint against the steel. When these sparks fell on the tinder, it began to glow and could be blown or fanned into flame.

venison. The flesh of animals of the deer family.

Index

(Page numbers in this Index that are preceded by "*p.*" refer to pictures.)